Thomas Wentworth Higginson

The Afternoon Landscape

Thomas Wentworth Higginson

The Afternoon Landscape

ISBN/EAN: 9783337720759

Printed in Europe, USA, Canada, Australia, Japan

Cover: Foto ©Andreas Hilbeck / pixelio.de

More available books at **www.hansebooks.com**

THE
AFTERNOON LANDSCAPE

Poems and Translations

BY

THOMAS WENTWORTH HIGGINSON

New York and London
LONGMANS, GREEN, AND CO.
1889

TO

JAMES RUSSELL LOWELL,

Schoolmate and Fellow-Townsman,

THIS BOOK IS INSCRIBED.

"Alter ab undecimo tum me jam ceperat annus,
 Jam fragiles poteram a terrâ contingere ramos."

"Ver erat aeternum; placidique tepentibus auris
 Mulcebant zephyri natos sine semine flores."

CAMBRIDGE, MASS., U. S. A.,
 1889.

CONTENTS.

[A few of these poems are by other hands, and are designated by initials.]

	PAGE
PRELUDE	9
SONNET TO DUTY	11
A JAR OF ROSE-LEAVES	12
SUB PONDERE CRESCIT	15
THE PLAYMATE HOURS	16
THE BABY SORCERESS	17
HEIRS OF TIME	18
SIXTY AND SIX: OR, A FOUNTAIN OF YOUTH	20
"SINCE CLEOPATRA DIED"	22
THE SOUL OF A BUTTERFLY	23
DECORATION	24
"THE SNOWING OF THE PINES"	26
THE LESSON OF THE LEAVES	27
VESTIS ANGELICA	28
TO MY SHADOW	30
TWO VOYAGERS	32
SEA-GULLS AT FRESH POND	33
THE DYING HOUSE	34
A SONG OF DAYS	37

	PAGE
TREASURE IN HEAVEN	38
BENEATH THE VIOLETS	40
"THE KNOCK ALPHABET"	41
THE REED IMMORTAL	42
DAME CRAIGIE	44
GIFTS	46
DWELLING-PLACES	48
TO THE MEMORY OF H. H.	49
VENUS MULTIFORMIS	50
TO JOHN GREENLEAF WHITTIER	52
PROLOGUE	53
CORPORAL ALSTON'S DISCOURSE	54
WAITING FOR THE BUGLE	56
ASTRA CASTRA	58
THE LAST PALATINE LIGHT	59
MEMORIAL ODE	64

EARLIER POEMS:

THE MADONNA DI SAN SISTO	71
HYMNS	73
POEMS FROM "THALATTA"	77
THE FEBRUARY HUSH	80
JUNE	81
DECEMBER	82
TO A YOUNG CONVERT	84
SERENADE BY THE SEA	86
THE FROZEN CASCADE	87
THE THINGS I MISS	88

Contents.

TRANSLATIONS: PAGE
   SAPPHO'S ODE TO APHRODITE 93
   SONNET FROM PETRARCH (123) 95
   SONNET FROM PETRARCH (128) 96
   SONNET FROM PETRARCH (134) 97
   SONNET FROM PETRARCH (223) 98
   SONNET FROM PETRARCH (251) 99
   SONNET FROM PETRARCH (253) 100
   SONNET FROM PETRARCH (261) 101
   SONNET FROM PETRARCH (302) 102
   SONNET FROM PETRARCH (309) 103
   SONNET FROM PETRARCH (314) 104
   SONNET FROM CAMOENS (42) 105
   SONNET FROM CAMOENS (186) 106

PRELUDE.

I DREAMED one night that the calm hosts of heaven
Had lost their changeless paths; and as I stood
Beside the latticed window, I could watch
Those strange, fair pilgrims wandering from their shrines.
Up to the zenith rose the moon, and paused;
Stars went and came, and waxed and waned again,
Then vanished into nothing; meteors pale
Stole, soft as wind-blown blossoms, down the night;
Till I awoke to find the cold gray morn
Hymning its lonely dirges through the pines.

Were it not better that the planets fail,
And every heavenly orbit wander wide,
Than that this human life, its years like stars,
Should miss the accustomed sequence of content?

All times are good; life's morning let us sing,
Its sunny noon, high noon, the whole world's pause,
Nor less that sweet decline which ends in eve.
Life were monotonous with its morning hours,
Came not the hurrying years to shift our mood,
Unfold an altered heaven and spread its glow
O'er the changed landscape of time's afternoon.

SONNET TO DUTY.

> Θεός τις ἔστ' ἐν ἡμῖν.
> EURIPIDES (*Fragm.*).

LIGHT of dim mornings; shield from heat and cold;
  Balm for all ailments; substitute for praise;
  Comrade of those who plod in lonely ways
  (Ways that grow lonelier as the years wax old);
Tonic for fears; check to the over-bold;
  Nurse, whose calm hand its strong restriction lays,
  Kind but resistless, on our wayward days;
  Mart, where high wisdom at vast price is sold;
Gardener, whose touch bids the rose-petals fall,
  The thorns endure; surgeon, who human hearts
  Searchest with probes, though the death-touch be given;
Spell that knits friends, but yearning lovers parts;
  Tyrant relentless o'er our blisses all; —
  Oh, can it be, thine other name is Heaven?

A JAR OF ROSE-LEAVES.

MYRIAD roses fade unheeded,
    Yet no note of grief is needed;
When the ruder breezes tear them,
Sung or songless, we can spare them.
But the choicest petals are
Shrined in some deep Orient jar,
Rich without and sweet within,
Where we cast the rose-leaves in.

Life has jars of costlier price
Framed to hold our memories.
There we treasure baby smiles,
Boyish exploits, girlish wiles,
All that made our early days
Sweeter than these trodden ways
Where the Fates our fortunes spin:
Memory, toss the rose-leaves in!

A Jar of Rose-Leaves.

What the jar holds, that shall stay;
Time steals all the rest away.
Cast in love's first stolen word,
Bliss when uttered, bliss when heard;
Maiden's looks of shy surprise;
Glances from a hero's eyes;
Palms we risked our souls to win:
Memory, fling the rose-leaves in!

Now more sombre and more slow
Let the incantation grow!
Cast in shreds of rapture brief,
Subtle links 'twixt hope and grief;
Vagrant fancy's dangerous toys;
Covert dreams, narcotic joys
Flavored with the taste of sin:
Memory, pour the rose-leaves in!

Quit that borderland of pain!
Cast in thoughts of nobler vein,
Magic gifts of human breath,
Mysteries of birth and death.

What if all this web of change
But prepare for scenes more strange;
If to die be to begin?
Memory, heap the rose-leaves in!

SUB PONDERE CRESCIT.

CAN this be he, whose morning footstep trod
    O'er the green earth as in a regal home?
Whose voice rang out beneath the skyey dome
Like the high utterance of a youthful god?
Now with wan looks and eyes that seek the sod,
    Restless and purposeless as ocean foam,
    Across the twilight fields I see him roam
With shoulders bowed, as shrinking from the rod.
Oh lift the old-time light within thine eyes!
    Set free the pristine passion from thy tongue!
    Strength grows with burdens; make an end of sighs.
Let thy thoughts soar again their mates among,
    And as yon oriole's eager matins rise,
    Abroad once more be thy strong anthem flung!

THE PLAYMATE HOURS.

DAWN lingers silent in the shade of night,
    Till on the gloaming Baby's laughter rings.
    Then smiling Day awakes, and open flings
    Her golden doors, to speed the shining flight
Of restless hours, gay children of the light.
    Each eager playfellow to Baby brings
    Some separate gift,— a flitting bird that sings
    With her; a waving branch of berries bright;
A heap of rustling leaves; each trifle cheers
    This joyous little life but just begun.
    No weary hour to her brings sighs or tears;
And when the shadows warn the loitering sun,
    With blossoms in her hands, untouched by fears,
    She softly falls asleep, and day is done.

M. T. H.

THE BABY SORCERESS.

OUR baby sits beneath the tall elm-trees,
    A wreath of tangled ribbons in her hands;
    She twines and twists the many-colored strands,
    A little sorceress, weaving destinies.
Now the pure white she grasps; now nought can please
    But strips of crimson, lurid as the brands
    From passion's fires, or yellow, like the sands
    That lend soft setting to the azure seas.
And so with sweet incessant toil she fills
    A summer hour, still following fancies new,
    Till through my heart a sudden terror thrills
Lest, as she weaves, her aimless choice prove true.
    Thank God, our fates proceed not from our wills!
    The Power that spins the thread shall blend the hue.

HEIRS OF TIME.

INSCRIBED TO EDWARD BELLAMY.

> Aucun homme ne peut aliéner sa souveraineté, parcequ'il ne peut abdiquer sa nature ou cesser d'être homme ; et de la souveraineté de chaque individu naît, dans la société, la souveraineté collective de tous ou la souveraineté du peuple, également inaliénable. — ABBÉ DE LA MENNAIS, *Le Livre du Peuple* (1837).

FROM street and square, from hill and glen
    Of this vast world beyond my door,
I hear the tread of marching men,
    The patient armies of the poor.

The halo of the city's lamps
    Hangs, a vast torchlight, in the air;
I watch it through the evening damps:
    The masters of the world are there.

Not ermine-clad or clothed in state,
    Their title-deeds not yet made plain;
But waking early, toiling late,
    The heirs of all the earth remain.

Some day, by laws as fixed and fair
As guide the planets in their sweep,
The children of each outcast heir
The harvest-fruits of time shall reap.

The peasant brain shall yet be wise,
The untamed pulse grow calm and still;
The blind shall see, the lowly rise,
And work in peace Time's wondrous will.

Some day, without a trumpet's call,
This news will o'er the world be blown:
"The heritage comes back to all!
The myriad monarchs take their own!"

SIXTY AND SIX:

OR,

A FOUNTAIN OF YOUTH.

Fons, delicium domus.
        MARTIAL.

JOY of the morning,
    Darling of dawning,
Blithe little, lithe little daughter of mine!
    While with thee ranging
    Sure I'm exchanging
Sixty of my years for six years like thine.
    Wings cannot vie with thee,
    Lightly I fly with thee
Gay as the thistle-down over the lea.
    Life is all magic,
    Comic or tragic,
Played as thou playest it daily with me.

    Floating and ringing,
    Thy merry singing

Comes when the light comes, like that of the birds.
    List to the play of it!
    That is the way of it;
All's in the music and nought in the words.
    Glad or grief-laden,
    Schubert or Haydn,
Ballad of Erin or merry Scotch lay;
    Like an evangel,
    Some baby-angel
Brought from sky-nursery stealing away.

    Surely I know it,
    Artist nor poet
Guesses my treasure of jubilant hours.
    Sorrows, what are they?
    Nearer or far, they
Vanish in sunshine, like dew from the flowers.
    Years, I am glad of them;
    Would that I had of them
More and yet more, while thus mingled with thine
    Age, I make light of it,
    Fear not the sight of it,
Time's but our playmate, whose toys are divine.

"SINCE CLEOPATRA DIED."

> " Since Cleopatra died,
> I have lived in such dishonor that the world
> Doth wonder at my baseness."

"SINCE Cleopatra died!" Long years are past,
    In Antony's fancy, since the deed was done.
    Love counts its epochs, not from sun to sun,
    But by the heart-throb. Mercilessly fast
Time has swept onward since she looked her last
    On life, a queen. For him the sands have run
    Whole ages through their glass, and kings have won
And lost their empires o'er earth's surface vast
Since Cleopatra died. Ah! Love and Pain
    Make their own measure of all things that be.
    No clock's slow ticking marks their deathless strain;
The life they own is not the life we see;
    Love's single moment is eternity:
    Eternity, a thought in Shakspeare's brain.

THE SOUL OF A BUTTERFLY.

OVER the field where the brown quails whistle,
    Over the ferns where the rabbits lie,
Floats the tremulous down of a thistle.
    Is it the soul of a butterfly?

See! how they scatter and then assemble;
    Filling the air while the blossoms fade, —
Delicate atoms, that whirl and tremble
    In the slanting sunlight that skirts the glade.

There goes the summer's inconstant lover,
    Drifting and wandering, faint and far;
Only bewailed by the upland plover,
    Watched by only the twilight star.

Come next August, when thistles blossom,
    See how each is alive with wings!
Butterflies seek their souls in its bosom,
    Changed thenceforth to immortal things.

DECORATION.

"Manibus O date lilia plenis."

Mid the flower-wreathed tombs I stand
    Bearing lilies in my hand.
Comrades! in what soldier-grave
Sleeps the bravest of the brave?

Is it he who sank to rest
With his colors round his breast?
Friendship makes his tomb a shrine;
Garlands veil it: ask not mine.

One low grave, yon trees beneath,
Bears no roses, wears no wreath;
Yet no heart more high and warm
Ever dared the battle-storm,

Decoration.

Never gleamed a prouder eye
In the front of victory,
Never foot had firmer tread
On the field where hope lay dead,

Than are hid within this tomb
Where the untended grasses bloom,
And no stone, with feigned distress,
Mocks the sacred loneliness.

Youth and beauty, dauntless will,
Dreams that life could ne'er fulfil,
Here lie buried; here in peace
Wrongs and woes have found release.

Turning from my comrades' eyes,
Kneeling where a woman lies,
I strew lilies on the grave
Of the bravest of the brave.

"THE SNOWING OF THE PINES."

SOFTER than silence, stiller than still air,
    Float down from high pine-boughs the slender leaves.
    The forest floor its annual boon receives
    That comes like snowfall, tireless, tranquil, fair.
Gently they glide, gently they clothe the bare
    Old rocks with grace. Their fall a mantle weaves
    Of paler yellow than autumnal sheaves
    Or those strange blossoms the witch-hazels wear.
Athwart long aisles the sunbeams pierce their way;
    High up, the crows are gathering for the night;
    The delicate needles fill the air; the jay
Takes through their golden mist his radiant flight;
    They fall and fall, till at November's close
    The snow-flakes drop as lightly — snows on snows.

THE LESSON OF THE LEAVES.

O THOU who bearest on thy thoughtful face
  The wearied calm that follows after grief,
 See how the autumn guides each loosened leaf
  To sure repose in its own sheltered place.
Ah, not forever whirl they in the race
  Of wild forlornness round the gathered sheaf,
  Or hurrying onward in a rapture brief
 Spin o'er the moorlands into trackless space.
Some hollow captures each; some sheltering wall
  Arrests the wanderer on its aimless way;
 The autumn's pensive beauty needs them all,
And winter finds them warm, though sere and gray.
  They nurse young blossoms for the spring's sweet call,
 And shield new leaflets for the burst of May.

VESTIS ANGELICA.

[IT was a custom of the early English church for pious laymen to be carried in the hour of death to some monastery, that they might be clothed in the habit of the religious order, and might die amid the prayers of the brotherhood. The garment thus assumed was known as the *Vestis Angelica*. See MORONI: *Dizionario di Erudizione Storico-Ecclesiastica*, ii. 78; xcvi. 212.]

O GATHER, gather! Stand
    Round her on either hand!
O shining angel-band
    More pure than priest!
A garment white and whole
Weave for this passing soul,
Whose earthly joy and dole
    Have almost ceased.

Weave it of mothers' prayers,
Of sacred thoughts and cares,
Of peace beneath gray hairs,
    Of hallowed pain;

Weave it of vanished tears,
Of childlike hopes and fears,
Of joys, by saintly years
    Washed free from stain.

Weave it of happy hours,
Of smiles and summer flowers,
Of passing sunlit showers,
    Of acts of love;
Of footsteps that did go
Amid life's work and woe, —
Her eyes still fixed below,
    Her thoughts above.

Then as those eyes grow dim
Chant we her best-loved hymn,
While from yon church-tower's brim
    A soft chime swells.
Her freed soul floats in bliss
To unseen worlds from this,
Nor knows in which it is
    She hears the bells.

TO MY SHADOW.

A MUTE companion at my side
    Paces and plods, the whole day long,
Accepts the measure of my stride,
Yet gives no cheer by word or song.

More close than any doggish friend,
Not ranging far and wide, like him,
He goes where'er my footsteps tend,
Nor shrinks for fear of life or limb.

I do not know when first we met,
But till each day's bright hours are done
This grave and speechless silhouette
Keeps me betwixt him and the sun.

To my Shadow.

They say he knew me when a child;
Born with my birth, he dies with me;
Not once from his long task beguiled,
Though sin or shame bid others flee.

What if, when all this world of men
Shall melt and fade and pass away,
This deathless sprite should rise again
And be himself my Judgment Day?

TWO VOYAGERS.

WHEN first I mark upon my child's clear brow
    Thought's wrestling shadows their new struggle keep,
  Read my own conflicts in her questions deep,
  My own remorse in her repentant vow,
My own vast ignorance in her "Why?" and "How?"
  When my precautions only serve to heap
  New burdens, and my cares her needs o'erleap,
Then to her separate destiny I bow.
So seem we like two ships, that side by side,
  Older and younger, breast the same rough main
  Bound for one port, whatever winds betide,
In solemn interchange of joy or pain.
  I may not hold thee back. Though skies be dark,
  Put forth upon the seas, O priceless bark!

SEA-GULLS AT FRESH POND.

O LAKE of boyish dreams! I linger round
   Thy calm, clear waters and thine altered shores
   Till thought brings back the plash of childhood's oars, —
Long hid in memory's depths, a vanished sound.
Alone unchanged, the sea-birds yet are found
   Far floating on thy wave by threes and fours,
   Or grouped in hundreds, while a white gull soars,
Safe, beyond gunshot of the hostile ground.
I am no nearer to those joyous birds
   Than when, long since, I watched them as a child;
   Nor am I nearer to that flock more wild,
Most shy and vague of all elusive things,
   My unattainable thoughts, unreached by words.
   I see the flight, but never touch the wings.

THE DYING HOUSE.

SHE is dead; her house is dying;
   Round its long-deserted door,
From the hillside and the moor,
Swell the autumn breezes sighing.
Closer to its windows press
Pine-tree boughs in mute caress;
Wind-sown seeds in silence come,
Root, and grow, and bud, and bloom;
Year by year, kind Nature's grace
Wraps and shields her dwelling-place.
She who loved all things that grew,
Talked with every bird that flew,
Brought each creature to her feet
With persuasive accents sweet, —
Now her voice is hushed and gone,
Yet the birds and bees keep on.

Oh the joy, the love, the glee,
Sheltered once by that roof-tree!
Song and dance and serenade,
Joyous jest by maskers played;
Passionate whispers on the stairs,
Hopes unspoken, voiceless prayers;
Greetings that repressed love's theme,
Partings that renewed its dream;
All the blisses, all the woes,
Youth's brief hour of spring-time knows, —
All have died into the past.
Perish too the house at last!

Vagrant children come and go
'Neath the windows, murmuring low;
Peering with impatient eye
For a ghostly mystery.
Some a fabled secret tell,
Others touch the soundless bell,
Then with hurrying step retreat
From the echo of their feet.
Or perchance there wander near
Guests who once held revel here:
Some live o'er again the days

Of their love's first stolen gaze;
Or some sad soul, looking in,
Calls back hours of blight or sin,
Glad if her mute life may share
In the sheltering silence there.
Oh, what cheeks might blanch with fears,
Had walls tongues, as they have ears!

Silent house with close-locked doors,
Ghosts and memories haunt thy floors!
Not a web of circumstance
Woven here into romance
E'er can perish; many a thread
Must survive when thou art dead.
Children's children shall not know
How their doom of joy or woe
Was determined ere their birth,
'Neath this roof that droops to earth,
By some love-tie here create,
Or hereditary hate,
Or some glance whose bliss or strife
Was the climax of a life,
Though its last dumb witness falls
With the crumbling of these walls.

A SONG OF DAYS.

O RADIANT summer day,
   Whose air, sweet air, steals on from flower
      to flower!
Couldst thou not yield one hour
When the glad heart says, "This alone is May"?

O passionate earthly love,
Whose tremulous pulse beats on to life's best boon!
Couldst thou not give one noon,
One noon of noons, all other bliss above?

O solemn human life,
Whose nobler longings bid all conflict cease!
Grant us one day's deep peace
Beyond the utmost rumor of all strife.

For if no joy can stay,
Let it at least yield one consummate bloom,
Or else there is no room
To find delight in love, or life, or May.

TREASURE IN HEAVEN.

IF messengers we fear
   Should hither come to-day,
   And beckon me away
From all that earth holds dear;

And I should trembling turn
   And cling to glowing life,
   Yet in the fiercest strife
Feel heart and reason burn;

Then look into love's face,
   And see with anguish wild
   Our rosy little child
With all her baby grace,

And stretch my feeble hand
   To keep the darling near, —
   My fainting soul would hear
A voice from spirit-land.

That voice would set me free,
   With joy my pulses thrill,
   "Mamma, I need you still!
Have you forgotten me?"

M. T. H.

1883.

BENEATH THE VIOLETS.

SAFE 'neath the violets
   Rests the baby form;
Every leaf that springtime sets
   Shields it from the storm.
Peace to all vain regrets
   Mid this sunshine warm!

Shadows come and shadows go
   O'er the meadows wide;
Twice each day, to and fro,
   Steals the river-tide;
Each morn with sunrise-glow
   Gilds the green hillside.

Peace that no sorrow frets
   In our souls arise!
Over all our wild regrets
   Arching, like the skies;
While safe 'neath the violets
   Sleep the violet eyes.

1880.

"THE KNOCK ALPHABET."

[Mr. KENNAN tells us that Russian prisoners converse with each other in a complex alphabet, indicated by knocking on the walls of their cells.]

LIKE prisoners, each within his own deep cell,
    We mortals talk together through a wall.
    "Was that low note indeed my brother's call?
    Or but a distant water-drop which fell?"
Yet to the straining ear each sound can tell
    Some woe that might the bravest heart appal,
    Or some high hope that triumphs over all:
    "Brother, I die to-morrow." "Peace!" "All's well!"
Oh, could we once see fully, face to face,
    But one of these our mates, — once speak aloud,
    Once meet him, heart to heart, in strong embrace, —
How would our days be glad, our hopes be proud!
    Perchance that wall is Life; and life being done,
    Death may unite these sundered cells in one.

THE REED IMMORTAL.

INSCRIBED TO THE BOSTON PAPYRUS CLUB.

[PLINY tells us that the Egyptians regarded the papyrus as an emblem of immortality.]

REED of the stagnant waters,
   Far in the Eastern lands,
Rearing thy peaceful daughters
   In sight of the storied sands!
Armies and fleets defying
   Have swept by that quiet spot,
But thine is the life undying,
   Theirs is the tale forgot.

The legions of Alexander
   Are scattered and gone and fled,
And the queen who ruled commander
   Over Antony, is dead;

The Reed Immortal.

The marching armies of Cyrus
   Have vanished in earth again,
And only the frail papyrus
   Still reigns o'er the sons of men.

Papyrus! O reed immortal,
   Survivor of all renown!
Thou heed'st not the solemn portal
   Where heroes and kings go down.
The monarchs of generations
   Have died into dust away;
O reed that outlivest nations,
   Be our symbol of strength to-day!

DAME CRAIGIE.

[LINES read at the Longfellow Memorial Reading, Cambridge, Feb. 27, 1888.]

IN childish Cambridge days, now long ago,
    When pacing schoolward in the morning hours,
I passed the stately homes of Tory Row
    And paused to see Dame Craigie tend her flowers.

Framed in the elm-tree boughs before her door
    The old escutcheon of our town was seen, —
Canker-worms *pendent*, yellowing leaves in *or*,
    School-boys *regardant*, on a field grass-green.

Dame Craigie, with Spinoza in her hand,
    Was once heard murmuring to the insect crew,
"I will not harm you, little restless band!
    For what are mortal men but worms, like you?"

The trees are gone; Dame Craigie too is gone,
 Her tongue long silent, and her turban furled;
Yet 'neath her roof thought's silk-worms still spun on,
 Whose sumptuous fabric clothed a barren world.

GIFTS.

A FLAWLESS pearl, snatched from an ocean
    cave,
  Remote from light or air,
And by the mad caress of stormy wave
  Made but more pure and fair;

A diamond, wrested from earth's hidden zone,
  To whose recesses deep
It clung, and bravely flashed a light that shone
  Where dusky shadows creep;

A sapphire, in whose heart the tender rays
  Of summer skies had met;
A ruby, glowing with the ardent blaze
  Of suns that never set, —

These priceless jewels shone, one happy day,
    On my bewildered sight:
"We bring from earth, sea, sky," they seemed to say,
    "Love's richness and delight."

"For me?" I trembling cried. "Thou need'st not dread,"
    Sang heavenly voices sweet;
And unseen hands placed on my lowly head
    This crown, for angels meet.

M. T. H.

DWELLING-PLACES.

WHERE is thy home, O little fair head,
    With thy sunny hair, on earth's clouded way?
"On my lover's breast; and I take my rest,
And I know no terror by night or day."

Where is thy home, O little fair heart,
With thy joyous hopes in life's shadows dim?
"In my lover's heart; and we never part,
For he carries me round the world with him."

Where is thy home, O little fair soul,
So brave 'mid the old world's sorrow and care?
"My home is in heaven. To me 't is given
To win my lover to meet me there."

TO THE MEMORY OF H. H.

O SOUL of fire within a woman's clay!
  Lifting with slender hands a race's wrong,
  Whose mute appeal hushed all thine early song,
  And taught thy passionate heart the loftier way, —
What shall thy place be in the realm of day?
  What disembodied world can hold thee long,
  Binding thy turbulent pulse with spell more strong?
Dwell'st thou, with wit and jest, where poets may,
Or with ethereal women (born of air
  And poet's dreams) dost live in ecstasy,
  Teach new love-thoughts to Shakespeare's Juliet fair,
New moods to Cleopatra? Then, set free,
  The woes of Shelley's Helen thou dost share,
  Or weep with poor Rossetti's Rose Mary.

VENUS MULTIFORMIS.

THREE men on a broken deck-plank,
    With the reef and its roar ahead,
Floated on, through a fair June morning,
    To a doom that was sure and dread.

Said one, "My years have been wasted
    On a woman's terrible charms;
But oh! to see death draw near me,
    And to die outside of her arms!"

Said another, "Through surge and through tempest
    My eyes are fixed on her face;
I forget the tumult of ocean
    In the joy of her last embrace."

Said the third, "I can die unflinching
    Wherever my fortune lies;
But oh! her endless bereavement,
    And the rivers of tears from her eyes!"

While the woman they all had worshipped
  Walked out from the gray church-door
Amid smiles and greetings and music,
  And followed by prayers of the poor.

TO JOHN GREENLEAF WHITTIER.

AT dawn of manhood came a voice to me
    That said to startled conscience, "Sleep no
        more!"
    Like some loud cry that peals from door to door
    It roused a generation; and I see,
Now looking back through years of memory,
    That all of school or college, all the lore
    Of worldly maxims, all the statesman's store,
    Were nought beside that voice's mastery.
If any good to me or from me came
    Through life, and if no influence less divine
    Has quite usurped the place of duty's flame;
If aught rose worthy in this heart of mine,
    Aught that, viewed backward, wears no shade
        of shame, —
    Bless thee, old friend! for that high call was
        thine.

CAMBRIDGE, Dec. 17, 1887.

PROLOGUE.

[RECITED by a young lady at the first performance of the Vassall House Dramatic Club, Cambridge, Mass., Dec. 8, 1882.]

BENEATH this roof the stately Vassall race
　　Once swept these halls in velvet and point-lace,
Sedately welcomed many an English lord,
And met him with the snuff-box, not the sword.
A hundred years are passed. We fill the scene
With humbler graces, less chivalric mien.
Yet you may see upon our mimic stage
The show and semblance of that earlier age;
The old brocades may veil some modern form
Of living beauty and of heart still warm;
And we, the youths and maidens of to-day,
Will be your vassals if you'll like our play.

CORPORAL ALSTON'S DISCOURSE.

SWIFT shooting down that Southern river's bends,
Like logs in freshet, swept our steamers on;
Their midships lumbered up with useless bales,
Old household stuffs and huddled clothes in rags,
And sombre groups of sleeping negroes, — waifs
Just taken on board from dug-outs, timbers, rafts,
Or off the rice-fields that spread either side,
One vast green chequer-work of dyke and pool.
Here the swart mothers and their babies dozed
'Mid all their earthly goods; and here and there
A silent sentinel watched a silent form
Wrapped in a blanket, nerveless, pulseless, cold,
Nigh to a dull red smear upon the plank,
Or splintered shot-hole in our ship's stout side.

But I, going past them to the forward deck,
Saw only squads of dusky soldiers, couched

Like some vast caravan, beneath the moon,
A breathing mass of black and ivory;
And o'er them all a high, shrill voice pealed forth
The burden of exhortation. I knew it well,
Old Adam Alston's voice; and thus it spoke:

"When I heard de bombshell screamin' troo de woods
Like de Judgment Day, I said widin myself,
'Suppose my head been took clean off dis night,
Dey could n't put my soul in de torments. No,
No! not perceps I hab for an enemy
De Mos' High God!' And when de bullets come,
Ho! dem dar bullets a-swishin' across de deck,
I cried aloud, 'Lord, help my congregation!
Boys, load and fire!'"

                Then rang the strong Amens
And bursts of laughter from glad African lungs;
Then all was still but one blithe mocking-bird
High on the bank, and that strange ominous fowl
The chuck-will's-widow, and our engine's throb;
While Southern fire-flies, twice as large as ours,
Swarmed from the meadows to the tree-tops high
And hung there, clustering Pleiads, earthly stars.

WAITING FOR THE BUGLE.

[READ before the Grand Army Post (56) of veteran soldiers, at Cambridge, Mass., May 25, 1888.]

WE wait for the bugle; the night-dews are cold,
The limbs of the soldiers feel jaded and old,
The field of our bivouac is windy and bare,
There is lead in our joints, there is frost in our hair,
The future is veiled and its fortunes unknown,
As we lie with hushed breath till the bugle is blown.

At the sound of that bugle each comrade shall spring
Like an arrow released from the strain of the string;
The courage, the impulse of youth shall come back
To banish the chill of the drear bivouac,

And sorrows and losses and cares fade away
When that life-giving signal proclaims the new day.

Though the bivouac of age may put ice in our veins,
And no fibre of steel in our sinew remains;
Though the comrades of yesterday's march are not here,
And the sunlight seems pale and the branches are sere, —
Though the sound of our cheering dies down to a moan,
We shall find our lost youth when the bugle is blown.

ASTRA CASTRA.

SOMEWHERE betwixt me and the farthest star,
  Or else beyond all worlds, all space, all thought,
  Dwells that freed spirit, now transformed and taught
To move in orbits where the immortals are.
Does she rejoice or mourn? Perchance from far
  Some earthly errand she but now has sought,
  By instantaneous ways among us brought,
Ways to which night and distance yield no bar.
Could we but reach and touch that wayward will
  On earth so hard to touch, would she be found
  Controlled or yet impetuous, free or bound,
Tameless as ocean, or serene and still?
  If in her heart one eager impulse stirs,
  Could heaven itself calm that wild mood of hers?

THE LAST PALATINE LIGHT.

[ONE of the best-known traditions of our Atlantic coast is that of the "Palatine Light," popularly associated with the wreck, off Block Island in 1720, of a ship bearing emigrants from the German Palatinates. The light is reported as appearing at irregular intervals for more than a century, and was last seen in 1832. Its appearance is minutely described by an eye-witness, a resident physician, who saw it Dec. 20, 1810. See SHEFFIELD: "Block Island," p. 42.]

ROGER HARLAKENDEN climbed the hill
   Where no other fisherman dared to go;
The east-wind was blowing bitter and chill,
   Sheer was the cliff and the footing slow;
Handgrip on rock and knee on the sod, —
At last on the headland's height he trod.

In the days of the pirates three footpaths led
   To that dizzy cliff; but now there was none
     Save for the fox, the goat, and the bird:
One path o'er the seaweeds green and red;
   From high-water mark to the cave-mouth, one;
     And thence o'er the Pirates' Hill, the third.

Roger Harlakenden threw him down,
   Breathless at last, on the thin dry grass;
He could see his dory that glistened brown,
   He could see the men and the women pass,
Tending the fish-flakes, from door to door;
And then he looked off to the ocean-floor.

Like a land-locked haven in sight of the sea
   The life of the twelvemonth past was spread;
   Peaceful contentment of heart and head
Since the Lord had found him, from sin set free.
Yet sometimes the thought of his wilder years
   Rushed back upon him, teeming with ill, —
Wicked joys and delicious fears;
   And then he climbed to the Pirates' Hill.

Was it worth the strength of a man like him
   To dwell by the bay, with a calm sweet wife;
No stir in the blood, no peril of limb,
   No wild, fierce joy of the coming strife?
Just to clean his boat and to haul the seines,
   To cook the fish by the drift-wood fire,
To play with his boy through the autumn rains,
   And on Sunday sing with his wife in the choir?

The Last Palatine Light.

Straight from the far horizon's line
The east-wind blew; the smell of the brine
  Banished the months of weary peace,
  And bade this desolate torpor cease.
It was almost sunset; there was the sea.
Only a night's hard pull, and he
  With his dory made fast to a whale-ship's side
  Could rock once more on the ocean wide.

What to him the fare or the men?
  The ruder the better. He held his own
    Still with the roughest. God! how he longed
    To be once more where the sailors thronged,
Or the old-time wreckers might shout again
  On some cruel isle of the middle zone!

See! with the sunset came once more
  The Palatine Light, the ship on fire!
  Each generation, son and sire,
Had watched it gleam, since the current bore
  The fated ship to a merciless wreck,
  With the crew in sight on the blazing deck.

There was the phantom now! the flame
  Climbed stay and halyard to pennon-staff!

There was neither pity nor joy nor shame
  In Roger Harlakenden's bitter laugh.
"Let it burn!" he said; "let the ocean roar!
I have looked on burning ships before.

"I will watch that light with a steadfast eye
  From this moment out, till the sun goes down;
If it lasts till the last red sunbeam, I
  Will be quit this night of the cursèd town!"
Then he tried to think of his wife and child;
But his lips grew stern, and the wind was wild.

Suddenly met him the startled face
Of a boy who had climbed to that dizzy place, —
  Half-triumphant and yet half-scared,
  But daring whatever his father dared.
The fisherman trembled, 'twixt wrath and fright.
  Terror next in that young voice rang:
  "Father!" it cried. Harlakenden sprang —
Out went the gleam of the Palatine Light!

He clasped the child in his strong embrace,
He thrust back the curls from the rosy face;
  Then faded the last bright flush of day,

The Last Palatine Light.

A shadow fell on the ocean-swells,
    And soft from the mainland dim and gray
Came the sweet, far sound of the Christmas bells.
    Never since then has a sailor seen
    The lurid wraith of the Palatine.

MEMORIAL ODE.

[READ before the Grand Army Posts of Boston, Mass., on Memorial Day, May 30, 1881, by Mr. George Riddle.]

I.

JOY to the three-hilled city! — for each year
Heals something of the grief this day records;
    Each year the plaintive lay
    Sounds yet more far away,
And strains of triumph suit memorial words.
The old-time pang becomes a thrill of joy;
    Again we turn the page
    Of our heroic age,
And read anew the tale of every patriot boy.
A modest courage was their simple wont,
The dauntless youths who grew to manhood here:
Putnam and Savage, Perkins and Revere.
    It needs no helmet's gleam,
    No armor's glittering beam,

No feudal imagery of shield or spear
To gild the gallant deeds that roused us then,—
When Cass fell dying in the battle's front,
And Shaw's fair head lay 'mid his dusky men.

II.

   All o'er the tranquil land
   On this Memorial Day,
     Coming from near and far,
Men gather in the mimic guise of war.
    They bear no polished steel,
Yet by the elbow's touch they march, they wheel,
    Or side by side they stand.
They now are peaceful men, fair Order's sons;
But as they halt in motionless array,
    Or bow their heads to pray,
     Into their dream intrudes
The swift sharp crack of rifle-shots in woods;
    Into their memory swells
The trumpet's call, the screaming of the shells;
And ever and anon they seem to hear
The far-off thunder of besieging guns,—
All sounds of bygone war, all memories of the ear.

III.

A little while it seems
Since those were daily thoughts which now are
dreams.
A little while is gone
Since, the last battle fought, the victory won,
We saw sweet Peace come back with all her
charms,
And watched a million men lay down their arms.
But at this morning's call
We bridge the interval;
And yet once more, with no regretful tears,
Live back again, though now men's blood be
cooled,
Through the long vista of the fading years
To days when Sumner spoke, and Andrew ruled.

IV.

Courage is first and last of what we need
To mould a nation for triumphal sway:
All else is empty air,
A promise vainly fair,
Like the bright beauty of the ocean spray

Tossed up toward heaven, but never reaching there.
Not in the past, but in the future, we
    Must seek the mastery
Of fate and fortune, thought and word and deed.
Gone, gone for aye, the little Puritan homes;
Gone the beleaguered town, from out whose spires
    Flashed forth the warning fires
Telling the Cambridge rustics, " Percy comes ! "
And gone those later days of grief and shame
When slavery changed our court-house to a jail,
And blood-drops stained its threshold. Now we
    hail,
    After the long affray,
A time of calmer order, wider aim,
More mingled races, manhood's larger frame,
A city's broader sweep, the Boston of to-day.

V.

They say our city's star begins to wane,
Our heroes pass away, our poets die,
Our passionate ardors mount no more so high.
'T is but an old alarm, the affright of wealth,
The cowardice of culture, wasted pain !
    Freedom is hope and health !

The sea on which yon ocean steamers ride
Is the same sea that rocked the shallops frail
Of the bold Pilgrims; yonder is its tide,
And here are we, their sons; it grows not pale,
Nor we who walk its borders. Never fear!
    Courage and truth are all!
Trust in the great hereafter, and whene'er
    In some high hour of need,
    That tests the heroic breed,
The Boston of the future sounds its call,
Bartletts and Lowells yet shall answer, "Here!"

EARLIER POEMS.

THE MADONNA DI SAN SISTO.

[THESE verses, written and published at the age of nineteen, are here preserved, partly from their association with my dear old friend and college teacher, Professor Longfellow, who liked them well enough to include them in his "Estray," in 1847.]

LOOK down into my heart,
    Thou holy Mother, with thy holy Son!
Read all my thoughts, and bid the doubts depart,
    And all the fears be done.

    I lay my spirit bare,
O blessèd ones! beneath your wondrous eyes,
And not in vain; ye hear my heartfelt prayer,
    And your twin-gaze replies.

    What says it? All that life
Demands of those who live, to be and do, —
Calmness, in all its bitterest, deepest strife;
    Courage, till all is through.

Thou Mother! in thy sight
Can aught of passion or despair remain?
Beneath those eyes' serene and holy light
    The soul is bright again.

Thou Son! whose earnest gaze
Looks ever forward, fearless, steady, strong;
Beneath those eyes no doubt or weakness stays,
    Nor fear can linger long.

Thanks, that to my weak heart
Your mingled powers, fair forms, such counsel give.
Till I have learned the lesson ye impart,
    I have not learned to live.

And oh, till life is done
Of your deep gaze may ne'er the impression cease!
Still may the dark eyes whisper, "Courage! On!"
    The mild eyes murmur, "Peace!"

HYMNS.

[THESE three hymns were written at the age of twenty-two, and were published anonymously in a collection edited by my friends Samuel Longfellow and Samuel Johnson. They are here inserted mainly because they have secured for themselves a semblance of permanent vitality in hymn-books, and are not always correctly printed.]

I.

I WILL ARISE AND GO UNTO MY FATHER.

TO Thine eternal arms, O God,
    Take us, Thine erring children, in;
From dangerous paths too boldly trod,
From wandering thoughts and dreams of sin.

Those arms were round our childish ways,
A guard through helpless years to be;
Oh leave not our maturer days,
We still are helpless without Thee!

We trusted hope and pride and strength:
Our strength proved false, our pride was vain,

Our dreams have faded all at length, —
We come to Thee, O Lord, again!

A guide to trembling steps yet be!
Give us of Thine eternal powers!
So shall our paths all lead to Thee,
And life smile on like childhood's hours.

II.

THE HOPE OF MAN.

THE Past is dark with sin and shame,
The Future dim with doubt and fear;
But, Father, yet we praise Thy name,
Whose guardian love is always near.

For man has striven, ages long,
With faltering steps to come to Thee,
And in each purpose high and strong
The influence of Thy grace could see.

He could not breathe an earnest prayer,
But Thou wast kinder than he dreamed,
As age by age brought hopes more fair,
And nearer still Thy kingdom seemed.

But never rose within his breast
A trust so calm and deep as now;
Shall not the weary find a rest?
Father, Preserver, answer Thou!

'T is dark around, 't is dark above,
But through the shadow streams the sun;
We cannot doubt Thy certain love;
And Man's true aim shall yet be won!

III.

PANTHEISM AND THEISM.

No human eyes Thy face may see,
No human thought Thy form may know;
But all creation dwells in Thee,
And Thy great life through all doth flow!

And yet, O strange and wondrous thought!
Thou art a God who hearest prayer,
And every heart with sorrow fraught
To seek Thy present aid may dare.

And though most weak our efforts seem
Into one creed these thoughts to bind,
And vain the intellectual dream
To see and know the Eternal Mind, —

Yet Thou wilt turn them not aside
Who cannot solve Thy life divine,
But would give up all reason's pride
To know their hearts approved by Thine.

So, though we faint on life's dark hill,
And thought grow weak, and knowledge flee,
Yet faith shall teach us courage still,
And love shall guide us on to Thee!

POEMS FROM "THALATTA."

[THE two poems which follow are from a volume called "Thalatta; a book for the Sea-side," edited by my friend Samuel Longfellow and myself in 1853.]

I.

CALM.

'TIS a dull, sullen day, — the dull beach o'er
  In rippling curves the ebbing ocean flows;
Along each tiny crest that nears the shore
  A line of soft green shadow rises, glides, and goes.

The tide recedes, — the flat smooth beach grows bare,
  More faint the low sweet plashing on my ears,
Yet still I watch the dimpling shadows fair,
  As each is born, glides, pauses, disappears.

What channel needs our faith except the eyes?
  God leaves no spot of earth unglorified;
Profuse and wasteful, lovelinesses rise;
  New beauties dawn before the old have died.

Trust thou thy joys in keeping of the Power
  Who holds these faint soft shadows in His hand;
Believe and live, and know that hour by hour
  Will ripple newer beauty to thy strand.

II.

THE MORNING MIST.

THE mist that like a dim soft pall was lying,
    Mingling the gray sea with the low gray sky,
Floats upward now; the sunny breeze is sighing,
    And Youth stands pale before his destiny:
        O passionate heart of Youth!
Each rolling wave with herald voice is crying;
Thou canst delay, but never shun replying,
It calls thee living or it calls thee dying,
Though beauty fade before the glare of truth.

Thou wanderest onward 'neath the solemn morning,
    It seems like mid-day ere the sun rides high,
The soft mist fades, whose shadowy adorning
    Wrapt in a dreamy haze the earth and sky;
        The Ocean lies before!
O thou art lost if thou discard the warning
To make hot Day more fair than fairest dawning,
Till eve look back serenely on the morning
When Youth stood trembling on the ocean-shore.

THE FEBRUARY HUSH.

SNOW o'er the darkening moorlands, —
    Flakes fill the quiet air;
Drifts in the forest hollows,
    And a soft mask everywhere.

The nearest twig on the pine-tree
    Looks blue through the whitening sky,
And the clinging beech-leaves rustle
    Though never a wind goes by.

But there's red on the wildrose berries,
    And red in the lovely glow
On the cheeks of the child beside me,
    That once were pale, like snow.

JUNE.

SHE needs no teaching, — no defect is hers;
    She stands in all her beauty 'mid the trees.
'Neath the tall pines her golden sunshine stirs
    And shifts and trembles with each passing breeze.
All the long day upon the broad green boughs
    Lieth the lustre of her lovely life,
    While too much drugged with rapture to carouse
Broods her soft world of insect-being rife.
So without effort or perplexing thought
    She comes to claim all homage as her own,
    Clad in the richest garments Nature wrought,
Melting the strongest with her magic zone.
    O wondrous June! our lives should be like thee,
    With such calm grace fulfilling destiny.

S. L. H.

DECEMBER.

THE evening sky unseals its quiet fountain,
    Hushing the silence to a drowsy rain;
It spreads a web of dimness o'er the plain
    And round each meadow tree;
Makes this steep river-bank a dizzy mountain,
    And this wide stream a sea.

Stealing from upper headlands of deep mist,
The dark tide bears its icebergs ocean bound,
White shapeless voyagers, by each other kissed,
    With rustling, ghostly sound;
The lingering oak-leaves sigh, the birches shiver,
Watching the wrecks of summer far and near,
Where many a dew-drop, frozen on its bier,
    Drifts down the dusky river.

I know thee not, thou giant elm, who towerest
With shadowy branches in the murky air;
And this familiar grove, once light and fair,
    Frowns, an Enchanted Forest.

December.

Couldst thou not choose some other night to moan,
    O hollow-hooting owl?
There needs no spell from thy bewildered soul;
    I 'm ghost enough alone.

TO A YOUNG CONVERT.

LULLED by sweet words and lured by saintly
    charms,
  I see thy weary, wandering steps begin
To enter where the Church spreads wide her arms,
  Arms that have clasped their many thousands in.

From turret-windows and from high-arched door
  Looks many a face of saint and martyr dear:
"Hail, Eve's lost daughter,[1] wanderer now no more!
  Earth's chill damp air shall never reach thee
    here!

"Here Dante, Bayard, Catherine knelt in prayer;
  Come in! their great remembrance makes us
    strong."
Oh, enter not! for peril haunts the air
  Which even the loveliest lips have breathed too
    long.

        [1] "Hevae filia exul."

To a Young Convert.

Come out upon the mountain tops with me!
  See the glad day break o'er their spires of blue!
There lies within those cloisters' tracery
  A deadlier poison than in dankest dew.

The Orient sun, that in that templed span
  Lit all of beauty saintliest eyes could see,
Still falls in blessing on the humblest man
  Who works for freedom with a soul set free.

In vain! thou canst not; yet thy cheeks grow pale
  While thy lips smile, and rapture lights thine eyes;
The tender fascinations slow prevail,
  And half thy life before the altar dies.

Will it die all? I know not. I can wait.
  The free air presses round the cloister door,
And I shall listen at that stern-barred gate
  To hear thy sweet voice pray for life once more.

1850.

SERENADE BY THE SEA.

[Set to music by M. Albert Pégou.]

O'ER the ocean vague and wide
　　Sleep comes with the coming tide.
Breezes lull my lady fair,
Cool her eyelids, soothe her hair,
While the murmuring surges seem
To float her through a world of dream.

Shadowy sloops are gliding in
Safe the harbor-bar within.
Silently each phantom pale
Drops the anchor, furls the sail.
She, meanwhile, remote from me
Drifts on sleep's unfathomed sea.

So may every dream of ill
Find its anchorage, and be still;
Sorrow furl its sails and cease
In this midnight realm of peace;
And each wandering thought find rest
In the haven of her breast!

THE FROZEN CASCADE.

THE BRIDE OF THE ROCK.

IN beauty perfected, with lavish grace,
   She casts herself about his rugged form,
With all her vesture on, of snowy white,
Nor left one pendant out, one dropping pearl.
Could she be fairer? Through her inmost veins
The warm sun searches, as for some weak spot;
But with a pride refined she smileth back:
"I gave myself in beauty to this Rock;
Ancient he is, and reverend and strong;
And I will fringe him with my snowy arms,
And lay my white cheek on his dark gray brow,
Nor ever melt for all thy beaming eyes!"

S. L. H.

THE THINGS I MISS.

AN easy thing, O Power Divine,
    To thank Thee for these gifts of Thine!
For summer's sunshine, winter's snow,
For hearts that kindle, thoughts that glow.
But when shall I attain to this, —
To thank Thee for the things I miss?

For all young Fancy's early gleams,
The dreamed-of joys that still are dreams,
Hopes unfulfilled, and pleasures known
Through others' fortunes, not my own,
And blessings seen that are not given,
And never will be, this side heaven.

Had I too shared the joys I see,
Would there have been a heaven for me?

The Things I Miss.

Could I have felt thy presence near,
Had I possessed what I held dear?
My deepest fortune, highest bliss,
Have grown perchance from things I miss.

Sometimes there comes an hour of calm;
Grief turns to blessing, pain to balm;
A Power that works above my will
Still leads me onward, upward still.
And then my heart attains to this, —
To thank Thee for the things I miss.

1870.

TRANSLATIONS.

SAPPHO'S ODE TO APHRODITE.

Ποικιλόθρον', ἀθάνατ' 'Αφρόδιτα.

BEAUTIFUL-THRONED, immortal Aphrodite!
    Daughter of Zeus, beguiler! I implore thee
Weigh me not down with weariness and anguish,
            O thou most holy!

Come to me now! if ever thou in kindness
Hearkenedst my words, — and often hast thou hearkened,
Heeding, and coming from the mansion golden
            Of thy great Father,

Yoking thy chariot, borne by thy most lovely
Consecrated birds, with dusky-tinted pinions,
Waving swift wings from utmost heights of heaven
            Through the mid-ether;

Swiftly they vanished, leaving thee, O Goddess!
Smiling, with face immortal in its beauty,
Asking why I grieved, and why in utter longing
        I had dared call thee;

Asking what I sought, thus hopeless in desiring,
'Wildered in brain, and spreading nets of passion —
Alas, for whom? and saidst thou, "Who has harmed thee?
        O my poor Sappho!

"Though now he flies, ere long he shall pursue thee;
Fearing thy gifts, he too in turn shall bring them;
Loveless to-day, to-morrow he shall woo thee,
        Though thou shouldst spurn him."

Thus seek me now, O holy Aphrodite!
Save me from anguish, give me all I ask for, —
Gifts at thy hand! And thine shall be the glory,
        Sacred Protector!

SONNET FROM PETRARCH (123).

"I' vidi in terra angélici costumi."

I once beheld on earth celestial graces
   And heavenly beauties scarce to mortals known,
   Whose memory yields nor joy nor grief alone,
   But all things else in clouds and dreams effaces.
I saw how tears had left their weary traces
   Within those eyes that once the sun outshone;
   I heard those lips, in low and plaintive moan,
   Breathe words to stir the mountains from their places.
Love, wisdom, courage, tenderness, and truth
   Made, in their mourning, strains more high and dear
   Than ever wove sweet sounds for mortal ear;
And heaven seemed listening in such saddest ruth
   The very leaves upon the bough to soothe,
   Such sweetness filled the blissful atmosphere.

SONNET FROM PETRARCH (128).

" O passi sparsi ; O pensiér vaghi e pronti."

O WANDERING steps! O vague and busy dreams!
  O changeless memory! O fierce desire!
  O passion strong! heart weak with its own fire;
  O eyes of mine! not eyes, but living streams;
O laurel boughs! whose lovely garland seems
  The sole reward that glory's deeds require;
  O haunted life! delusion sweet and dire,
  That all my days from slothful rest redeems;
O beauteous face! where Love has treasured well
  His whip and spur, the sluggish heart to move
  At his least will; nor can it find relief.
O souls of love and passion! if ye dwell
  Yet on this earth, and ye, great Shades of Love!
  Linger, and see my passion and my grief.

SONNET FROM PETRARCH (134).

"Quando Amór i begli occhi a terra inchina."

WHEN Love doth those sweet eyes to earth incline,
   And weaves those wandering notes into a sigh
   With his own touch, and leads a minstrelsy
   Clear-voiced and pure, angelic and divine, —
He makes sweet havoc in this heart of mine,
   And to my thoughts brings transformation high,
   So that I say, "My time has come to die,
   If fate so blest a death for me design."
But to my soul thus steeped in joy the sound
   Brings such a wish to keep that present heaven,
   It holds my spirit back to earth as well.
And thus I live: and thus is loosed and wound
   The thread of life which unto me was given
   By this sole Siren who with us doth dwell.

SONNET FROM PETRARCH (223).

"Qual donna attende a gloriosa fama."

DOTH any maiden seek the glorious fame
    Of chastity, of strength, of courtesy?
    Gaze in the eyes of that sweet enemy
    Whom all the world doth as my lady name!
How honor grows, and pure devotion's flame,
    How truth is joined with graceful dignity,
    There thou mayst learn, and what the path may be
To that high heaven which doth her spirit claim;
There learn that speech beyond all poet's skill,
    And gracious silence, and those holy ways
    Unutterable, untold by human heart.
But the infinite beauty that all eyes doth fill,
    This none can learn! because its lovely rays
    Are given by God's pure grace, and not by art.

SONNET FROM PETRARCH (251).

" Gli occhi di ch' io parlái."

THOSE eyes, 'neath which my passionate rapture rose,
  The arms, hands, feet, the beauty that erewhile
  Could my own soul from its own self beguile,
  And in a separate world of dreams enclose;
The hair's bright tresses, full of golden glows,
  And the soft lightning of the angelic smile
  That changed this earth to some celestial isle, —
  Are now but dust, poor dust, that nothing knows.
And yet I live! Myself I grieve and scorn,
  Left dark without the light I loved in vain,
  Adrift in tempest on a bark forlorn;
Dead is the source of all my amorous strain,
  Dry is the channel of my thoughts outworn,
  And my sad harp can sound but notes of pain.

SONNET FROM PETRARCH (253).

" Soléasi nel mio cor."

SHE ruled in beauty o'er this heart of mine,
    A noble lady in a humble home;
    And now her time for heavenly bliss has come,
'T is I am mortal proved, and she divine.
The soul that all its blessings must resign,
    And love whose light no more on earth finds
        room
    Might rend the rocks with pity for their doom,
    Yet none their sorrows can in words enshrine;
They weep within my heart; no ears they find
    Save mine alone, and I am crushed with care,
    And nought remains to me save mournful breath.
Assuredly but dust and shade we are,
    Assuredly desire is mad and blind,
    Assuredly its hope but ends in death.

SONNET FROM PETRARCH (261).

" Levommi il mio pensiero."

DREAMS bore my fancy to that region where
    She dwells whom here I seek, but cannot see.
'Mid those who in the loftiest heaven be
    I looked on her, less haughty and more fair.
She took my hand; she said, "Within this sphere,
    If hope deceive not, thou shalt dwell with me:
    I filled thy life with war's wild agony;
Mine own day closed ere evening could appear.
My bliss no human thought can understand;
    I wait for thee alone, and that fair veil
    Of beauty thou dost love shall yet retain."
Why was she silent then, why dropped my hand
    Ere those delicious tones could quite avail
    To bid my mortal soul in heaven remain?

SONNET FROM PETRARCH (302).

"Gli angeli eletti."

THE holy angels and the spirits blest,
    Celestial bands, upon that day serene
    When first my love went by in heavenly sheen,
    Came thronging, wondering at the gracious guest.
"What light is here, in what new beauty drest?"
    They said among themselves "for none has seen
    Within this age arrive so fair a mien
    From changing earth unto immortal rest."
And she, contented with her new-found bliss,
    Ranks with the perfect in that upper sphere,
    Yet ever and anon looks back on this
To watch for me, as if for me she stayed.
    So strive my thoughts, lest that high heaven I miss;
    I hear her call, and must not be delayed.

SONNET FROM PETRARCH (309).

" Dicemi spesso il mio fidato speglio."

OFT by my faithful mirror I am told,
    And by my mind outworn and altered brow,
My earthly powers impaired and weakened
    now, —
" Deceive thyself no more, for thou art old !"
Who strives with Nature's laws is over-bold,
    And Time to his commandment bids us bow.
    Like fire that waves have quenched, I calmly vow
In life's long dream no more my sense to fold.
And while I think, our swift existence flies,
    And none can live again earth's brief career, —
    Then in my deepest heart the voice replies
Of one who now has left this mortal sphere,
    But walked alone through earthly destinies,
    And of all women is to fame most dear.

SONNET FROM PETRARCH (314).

"Dolci durezze e placide repulse."

GENTLE severity, repulses mild,
    Full of chaste love and pity sorrowing;
    Graceful rebukes, that had the power to bring
    Back to itself a heart by dreams beguiled;
A tender voice, whose accents undefiled
    Held sweet restraints, all duty honoring;
    The bloom of virtue; purity's sweet spring
    To cleanse away base thoughts and passions wild;
Divinest eyes to make a lover's bliss,
    Whether to bridle in the wayward mind
    Lest its wild wanderings should the pathway miss,
Or else its griefs to soothe, its wounds to bind, —
    This sweet completeness of thy life it is
    Which saved my soul; no other peace I find.

SONNET FROM CAMOENS (42).

[Mrs. Browning in "Catarina to Camoens" represents her as bequeathing him the ribbon from her hair; but she in reality gave it to him during her life as a substitute for the ringlet for which he pleaded.]

"*Lindo e subtil trançado, que ficaste.*"

O RIBBON fair, that dost with me remain
   In pawn for that sweet gift I do deserve,
   If but to win thee makes my reason swerve,
   What were it if one ringlet I could gain?
Those golden locks thy circling knots restrain,
   Locks whose bright rays might well for sunbeams serve,
   When thou unloosest each fair coil and curve,
   Oh is it to beguile, or slay with pain?
Dear ribbon, in my hand I hold thee now;
   And were it only to assuage my grief,
   Since I can have thee only, cling to thee,
Yet tell her, thou canst never fill my vow,
   But in the reckoning of love's fond belief
   This gift for that whole debt a pledge shall be.

SONNET FROM CAMOENS (186).

*For we had been reading Camoens, — that poem, you remember,
Which his lady's eyes were praised in, as the sweetest ever seen.*
      ELIZABETH BARRETT BROWNING.

" Os olhos onde o casto Amor ardia."

THOSE eyes from whence chaste love was wont to glow,
 And smiled to see his torches kindled there;
 That face within whose beauty strange and rare
The rosy light of dawn gleamed o'er the snow;
That hair, which bid the envious sun to know
 His brightest beams less golden rays did wear;
 That pure white hand, that gracious form and fair:
All these into the dust of earth must go.
O perfect beauty in its tenderest age!
 O flower cut down ere it could all unfold
 By the stern hand of unrelenting death!
Why did not Love itself quit earth's poor stage,
 Not because here dwelt beauty's perfect mould,
 But that so soon it passed from mortal breath?

FINIS.

www.ingramcontent.com/pod-product-compliance
Lightning Source LLC
Chambersburg PA
CBHW020152170426
43199CB00010B/996